I0475510

Book 1
Drawing
By Scott Landowski

&

Book 2
Pastel Drawing
By Scott Landowski

Book 1
Drawing

By Scott Landowski

1-2-3 Easy Techniques To Mastering Drawing

Drawing: 1-2-3 Easy Techniques to Mastering Drawing

Copyright 2017 by Scott Landowski - All rights reserved.

In no way is it legal to reproduce, duplicate, or transmit any part of this document in either electronic means or in printed format. Recording of this publication is strictly prohibited and any storage of this document is not allowed unless with written permission from the publisher. All rights reserved.

Table of Contents

Introduction

I want to thank you and congratulate you for downloading the book, "Drawing: 1-2-3 Easy Techniques to Mastering Drawing".

This book contains proven steps and strategies on how to master drawing as a beginner artist. You will learn three basic techniques for sketching just about any subject you can think of. These are lines, shading and proportion - that's it!

Anyone can draw. They just need a bit of guidance to know how they can use simple lines and curves to capture the world on paper. There is an artist in each one of us and the tips in this book will help unleash him or her. Start with these techniques and you can move on to creating an art in any medium including painting and digital drawing.

What is important is that you have a good, solid foundation before experimenting with art. After that, you will only be limited by your imagination.

Thank again for downloading this book,   I hope you enjoy it!

Chapter 1 - Working with the Right Materials

Like with any other craft, drawing requires the right materials. It is best to choose artist grade and good quality tools, but there are also less expensive options at the art store that can give you real value for your money. Learn to experiment with various brands and types to find the ones that suit you and your drawing style best. There are many wonderful artists who can create beautiful works of art with simple and cheap art tools.

Pencils

Graphite Pencils

First, in order to begin sketching, you must have pencils. You cannot just have any pencil. You need to invest in those with different hardness. The most commonly used type of pencil in sketching is the graphite pencil. Others incorrectly refer to the grey graphite encased inside the wood as lead, when in fact, it has long been banned for use in pencils because it is toxic.

The hardness of a graphite pencil is denoted by a grade that ranges from 9B to 9H. The "B" stands for "black" or graphite that is softer, while "H" stands for graphite that is "harder." The B graphite looks darker while the H graphite is lighter. The HB graphite is the middle ground and it is an absolute must to have. It corresponds to the #2 pencil of more mainstream pencil brands. For sketching, it is often enough to have 5 different pencil grades at your disposal. That is enough to provide different tones and shadows to your drawing.

Other wood pencils can also have colored pigments, or what is pertained to as colored pencils. These, along with graphite pencils, are sharpened using a sharpener that fits the circumference of the pencil.

Mechanical Pencils

You can also use mechanical pencils. These come with barrels that you can refill with graphite of different diameters often denoted by a point millimeter size. You can push out the graphite by pressing a button without the need to sharpen the pencil. They are also excellent for drawing fine details as they retain their point and do not easily become blunt unlike wood pencils.

Pastels

Charcoal and chalk pastels produce colors that are more vivid. They are more blendable than graphite pencils and are also more difficult to control due to their size and softness.

Erasers

Erasers are also just as important as pencils. You can use them not just to correct errors, but to also add highlights and depth to your drawing. Avoid using the eraser found in the body of your pencil. It is often of poor quality and will cause your paper to tear easily. Also, due to its small size, you will quickly grind it down to the wood. A normal rubber eraser will be useful if you want to erase large areas, but you will realize that you will rarely need to do that. If you really do not like your work, it is best to start with a clean sheet of paper. Rubber erasers also create a lot of mess from the grit formed when rubbing them on paper with graphite.

The dust can affect your work and make it dirty. The kneaded artist eraser is much better because it takes off graphite marks without damaging the paper. The eraser lasts longer because rubber bits do not fall off when erasing. You can also erase in layers, which is useful if an area simply needs brightening or highlighting. You can further mold it smaller and pointier to do detail work. As well, a mechanical eraser can target small areas because of its size. You can even sharpen it with a craft knife to create a pointed eraser.

Blenders

Blending tools can help achieve more realistic drawings. The most common is a blending stump, which is a paper or felt cylinder that has been tightly rolled up with pointed ends. Q-tips also serve a similar purpose, but they are meant to be disposable and you cannot use one piece several times. Wads of cotton, paper napkins and fabrics can also be used as blending tools.

Ink

An alternative to sketching with pencils is to use ink. There are even more types of drawing pens than there are pencils. There are artist pens with different millimeter diameters. There are also different types of tips like fine, blunt or scroll (two-tipped). Brush pens, calligraphic pens, nib pens and even markers create various effects in drawing. You can also use a wet brush to spread the ink and color in your drawing. The downside to working with ink is that you can no longer erase your marks. Some artists prefer to draw in pencil first then trace over in ink.

Paper

Drawing paper can greatly affect the outcome of your drawing. However, your choice of brand all comes down to your personal preference. Some prefer paper with pronounced teeth for texture. The teeth refers to the grain of the paper. Pigments stick better to such paper, although the point of your drawing apparatus may also get caught on the teeth. On the other hand, there are those who prefer the look and feel of smoother paper. If you are overwhelmed by the number of paper choices at your disposal, then try to look for paper that was created precisely for pencil sketching.

Watercolor paper also usually makes a good medium for sketching. Avoid paper for acrylics or oils, as well as paper that is similar to fabric like felt and canvas. There are also drawing pads or journals that you can take with you as you travel. Some may prefer to just use notebooks with heavy paper stock for practice drawings.

If you want your drawings to last, you may also want to get a can of fixative. These are usually sprays and they help preserve your drawings. Over time, graphite may transfer or move on the paper, the paper may begin to age and moisture may start to affect the integrity of your drawing. A fixative acts as a protection from possible wear and tear. Think of it as a varnish or a top coat to seal in your work. Remember to purchase a fixative designed mainly for pencils or inks and not for other art media.

Chapter 2 - Warm Up Exercises

If you thought that warming up is just done before physical exercise, then you may be surprised to find out that you must also do warm ups before drawing. You do this to help loosen up your hand and allow you to practice your strokes before doing actual sketching.

Grip

First, warm up exercises help reorient you on how to hold your pencil properly. Many people are used to gripping their pencil for sketching the way they do for writing where it is nestled on top of the gap between their thumb and forefinger, so the bottom is pointing up. This is called the tripod grip. The best way to hold your pencil for sketching is to position it underneath the palm of your hand in what is called the overhand grip. This type of grip is looser and allows you bigger movement that comes from your entire arm rather than just your wrist. Also, you will not be smudging your paper because your hand hovers on top of the paper.

Doodles

Start by doing slanted lines. Quickly draw lines that move diagonally up then diagonally down. Do rows of this and draw them as fast as you can, then as close together as possible. Make them even and the same size every time.

Sketch hatches that are crossed horizontal and vertical lines.

Next, draw curved lines or Cs. Draw them forward, then in reverse. Just like the slanted lines, make them even and in rows.

From there, move on to doing spirals or ovals one on top of the other. Draw rows of perfect circles afterwards.

Draw 3D shapes. You can start by sketching cubes. Shade the exposed surfaces in different tones to practice your shading and shadows.

Sketch cylinders and bowls and shade them in using curved strokes, as well. Do the same for cones.

Contour Drawing

Also, do some contour drawing. Pick an object and draw its outline without lifting your pencil off your paper. This teaches you to pay attention to the shape of the object you are drawing. Some artists also like doing this exercise without looking at their paper, so their full attention is on the subject itself. If you want to have a bit more challenge, turn your back from your paper and draw without looking back. This is best done on a large paper like an A3 size. This exercise is what you call a blind contour.

Drawing: 1-2-3 Easy Techniques to Mastering Drawing

Do not be occupied with making your warm up drawings perfect. You can just do them on scratch paper and sketch as many exercises as you want, although you also need to start practicing control. Remember that you are not simply doing. The warm up exercises are more purposeful than that and they will help you perform your strokes better later on when you are already doing actual sketches.

Chapter 3 - Choosing Subjects

Even though you want to draw abstract art or highly stylized figures, it is still important to learn how to draw objects realistically. This will teach you proper proportions and shadows. Once you have mastered realistic drawing, you will be able to break conventions and develop your own style.

Still Life

Beginner art classes usually start by sketching still life, which refers to small inanimate objects. You can just find random objects lying around your home or inside your bag. Try to find a combination of different textures, shapes and sizes. For example, a towel, bottle and fruits will allow you to practice drawing different types of objects. Also, make sure to arrange them in a way that they occupy different levels (i.e., high and low) and depths of fields (i.e., foreground, middle ground and background). This will teach you scale and perspective.

The most important thing to focus on when drawing still life is shape. For instance, an apple is just a circle with slight curves to make it look distinct from an orange. Likewise, a bottle is just a cylinder while a towel is just a polygonal shape. Once you can see shapes in real life, then it will be easier to capture how objects look in your sketches.

From small objects, you can move on to larger things like furniture or even entire rooms. The practice in perspective will also help you transition to doing landscapes.

Landscape

What is most important in landscape is perspective. You may have seen landscape paintings where most of the details are blurred. This is completely understandable, because when you are drawing something vast like a mountain view or an urban jungle, you won't be able to draw all the small parts. The observer won't notice these in real life when they are looking at the bigger picture. However, when there is something off with your perspective, then the illusion of realism is shattered.

For example, a tree close to the viewer should be bigger than a large mountain that is miles away. Amateur artists who do not pay attention to what they can actually see in the world may not realize this because in real life, trees are much smaller than mountains, but sometimes, what you think is logical does not really match reality.

Figure Drawing

This is especially true when drawing people. You may instinctively think that your leg is longer than your arm when they are actually the same length. Your

11

ears are also not high on your head but right in the middle of it at the same level as your nose.

Some artists start with statues, so you can go to an art gallery or a park where there are busts and sculptures. Look for subjects with realistic proportions. Again, focus on the shapes that you can find in a human body. The head is a circle while the limbs are cylinders. Spend more time on getting the actual figure or overall shape of the subject before learning how to draw the fingers, toes and facial features. Portraits or faces are typically the last type of drawings that artists master.

Next, you can practice drawing actual people. You can have a model sit down for a session or discreetly draw strangers sitting down in a public place.

There are places that offer figure drawing sessions with professional models. Some do nude modeling, which is beneficial for artists who want to understand fully how the human body looks.

Gesture Drawing

Gesture drawings are done quickly, usually in short intervals of 15, 30 or 60 seconds, with the use of expressive lines and shapes. They serve as starting points for different genres of art that do not rely on hyper-realistic figures like impressionism. Gesture drawings focus on the basic form and proportion of a subject and record that without much emphasis on details. They are good for practicing speed and expressing movement in drawing. Erasing is rarely done and mistakes give the drawing even more character.

The subject of a gesture drawing can be any object in motion like moving persons, animals, cars, boats and toys. The best place to find subjects is outdoors where there are lots of activities. You can watch a busy intersection and try to draw different kinds of people walking about and dodging cars. In a park, you can draw joggers with their dogs or children playing with their toys.

Chapter 4 - Easy Technique 1 - Lines

For any drawing that you do, you can start with an H pencil to create light outlines and follow up with a B pencil for the darker, more defined lines. However, you can also simply use just one pencil and vary your pressure as you draw more layers of lines. Also, the point of your pencil, especially when freshly sharpened, will create thin, light lines.

On the other hand, the side of your pencil will create thick, dark lines. You can also make the point blunt by rubbing it on another piece of paper. If you want to just use one pencil, instead of switching between H and B pencils, then use an HB or #2 pencil as described in Chapter 1.

So, your drawing should have at least two layers of lines: the first light outline, which you can use as a guideline to capture the basic shapes of the subject, and thicker lines on top of that to form the rest of your drawing.

For the first layer of lines, try to use a light pressure when pressing down on your pencil and use only light strokes. The fainter you make the lines, the better. They will be easier to erase later on if you have to.

The layer on top of the outline will use heavy lines. You can trace over the light outline, then vary your pressure and strokes as you go along to create more definition to your figure. Define the edges and the details. At this point, you want to be more careful as erasing may be more difficult to do on thick, dark lines. Even if you can lift the marks off your paper, the indentations may still be obvious and they may show up more if you draw over them.

You can also go over your final pencil outlines with ink and erase the pencil lines for a more polished look.

In drawing, it is impossible to create perfectly straight lines, so do not worry if your tables or boxes have crooked edges. The only way to achieve truly straight lines is to use a ruler, although dragging or rolling your pencil on its edge, instead of using the point, will help achieve straighter lines. Also, imperfect lines give your drawings more life and expression. Perfectly straight lines are also difficult to find in nature and in real life. Even buildings or straight poles have curves and small dips on their edges. That is why a drawing that makes use of straight lines looks cold, stiff and lifeless. It looks rather unrealistic and uninteresting.

Lines and Values

Drawings are made up of lines and clusters of lines or values. Lines are the flowing strokes of a pencil that define edges or small details while values are used to define the form and design of a drawing. Using both will give your drawings character.

The term value is sometimes used interchangeably with the terms "shade", "tint" and "tone." These terms are most useful when working with colored pencils.

Shade refers to the color achieved when black is combined with a pure color. You can do this to darken colors. For example, ultramarine, navy blue and midnight blue are shades of blue.

Tint refers to the color achieved when white is combined with a pure color. You can do this to lighten colors. For example, pink, rose and coral are tints of red.

Tone refers to the color achieved when grey is combined with a pure color. For example, khaki, brown and gold are tones of yellow.

However, when drawing with grey graphite pencils, these will all just fall under "value." Knowing if a color is a shade, tint or tone will allow you to adjust the values in your drawings to depict the color of your subject even in a black and white drawing. You simply need to look at the darkness or lightness of the greys you are using. A pink-colored blouse will look like a light grey while dark blue denim jeans will look almost black.

Furthermore, take note that value is different from the concept of shading, which will be discussed in Chapter 4. So for this chapter, only look at the "color" of the lines you are making

Value Scale

A value scale is extremely helpful to beginner artists. This will serve as a guide so you can tell what value you can use for different parts of your drawing. Most find a ten-point value scale to be adequate. You can make one on a piece of paper by drawing ten circles or squares. Fill the first one with the lightest stroke you can create with your pencil or with your lightest pencil. Next, fill the last one with the darkest stroke you can create with your pencil or with your darkest pencil.

Fill the rest with the remaining values in between going from the lightest to the darkest value. Use this scale as a guide that you can compare parts of your drawing to, so the heaviest outline should match the last value while faint edges should match the first value. Medium colors should match the two middle values.

By using values, you can also adjust the contrast of your drawing. A high contrast drawing will make more use of values at each end of the spectrum - almost black to almost white. Low contrast drawings will use a good mix of the whole spectrum. Whichever variation in value that you choose is completely up to you and will depend on the effect that you want to achieve. Your drawing can be harsh, bold and solid or soft, faint and hazy.

Thick and Thin Lines

The quickest way to achieve various values in your drawing is to vary the thickness of your lines. Thin lines represent the light values while thick lines represent the dark values. You can get different thicknesses by simply varying your pressure, using pencil points with different dullness, or using different pencils.

Scribbling

Scribbling is a good way to fill a space with a lot of values in a short period of time. It is quick and you can create hundreds of strokes in a minute. More advanced artists can create drawings made up of just scribbles and the subject will still remain clear to the viewer. Beginner artists may try this technique and just end up with a bunch of scribbles that do not look like anything. Again, focusing on the shape of the subject will give you a general guideline for where to lay down the scribbles on your paper.

You do scribbling by drawing a continuous series of lines that go in different directions. The sensation you should feel when scribbling is comparable to writing in longhand or cursive. Control the value by varying speed, pressure and distance between the scribbles. For example, when doing a portrait using the scribbling technique, the dark and closely overlapping scribbles will be concentrated on the subject's features like his hair, eyebrows, eyes, nose, mouth and general outline of the face.

Some scribbles may be used to define cheekbones, the sides of the nose and around the mouth where shadows fall on the face. Lastly, very faint scribbles can depict highlights on the face like the apples of the cheeks, the pupil and whites of the eyes, and shine of the lips and hair.

Side Strokes

Side strokes is a favorite among sketchers who do fast and loose drawings. They are especially good for achieving different values than for plain contour drawings. Short, sideways strokes will create different values of greys depending on the pressure, closeness of the lines and overlapping.

Wide Strokes

Wide strokes are good if you want to try getting a general impression of a subject. You use big, long (not necessarily dark) lines. Whereas side strokes are short lines, wide strokes take up more space in a short period of time. So, they are often used for large subjects like the full figure of a person or a wide landscape. You can also use them when getting the general movement or shape of a large portion of the drawing such as the drape of a fabric or hair flowing in the wind. It takes a lot of confidence to achieve wide strokes because it can sometimes make or break the foundation of your entire drawing.

Charcoal pencils or pastels are great to use when trying to achieve wide strokes, because these take less effort to get broad lines. They also go on paper smoothly

15

and don't catch on the "teeth" of the paper, which sometimes happens when drawing wide strokes with graphite pencils.

Single Strokes

Single strokes are simply straight lines drawn in a row. This is best done with a sharp pencil and each area is filled with parallel lines. Values are achieved by varying the density of the lines or how close the group of lines are to each other. The farther away the lines are, the lighter the value. It is a refined technique and is not as loose as the previous types of line drawings. It does create a similar effect with scribbling, except more polished.

However, it takes precision because one line that is not in its right place or a bit more crooked than the other will easily stand out and catch the attention of the viewer. Beginner artists should practice using this technique just to learn patience and meticulousness in drawing. It is good to use as a counter-balance to other stroke techniques. It is also best used for drawings that require precision like architecture.

Smudging and Erasing

After scribbling or doing side strokes, you can smudge the lines with your finger or other blender tools mentioned in Chapter 1. This will soften or smoothen the harsh lines. It is also a good technique to use when trying to achieve medium values. However, some artists avoid this technique because it does not teach how to achieve values properly using only lines. Also, smudging can get quite messy, which can ruin an already good drawing. It may be a form of cheating, but when done right or with some caution, you can enhance the drawing.

Another way to achieve lighter values is by erasing. This creates highlights or contrasting definition to some parts of a drawing. Sometimes, it is easier to just erase a portion filled with darker values than to avoid drawing on that spot or trying to achieve the lightest value you can.

Chapter 5 - Easy Technique 2 - Shading

Shading is another important technique in drawing. They give your sketches life and depth because they mimic the light and shadows found in the real world.

The progression of shading or values from light to dark or dark to light are called graduations. Graduated shading is important so that there is a good transition from one value to another. Beginner artists may jump from one value to another without proper graduation and this creates harsh, unrealistic shadows in their drawings. This is only acceptable when one is trying to create an obvious contrast between different portions of a drawing. For instance, the edge of an object should be distinguishable from its background; otherwise, the object will disappear.

Graduations can be done through a variation of strokes, pressure or pencil hardness. Continuously adjust the changes in values so that the transitions are not apparent. There should be no demarcations or borders that separate two or more values in a graduated shading. Adjust any areas that look irregular.

If you are just starting to experiment with graduation in drawing, you should being from the lightest shading to the darkest. It is much easier to build up on the color of a grey pencil than it is to remove an already dark color to make it lighter.

Light Source

Always identify where the light source of your subject is. When you do not consider where the light is coming from, your drawing will look two dimensional. For example, when drawing an outdoor scene, take note of where the sun is depending on the time of day. Noon time creates solid shadows that are short and go straight down from the objects. The lower the sun in the sky is (especially at the beginning and at the end of the day), the longer and fainter the shadows are. They will also slant at different directions. When it comes to drawing still life indoors, take notice of where the window is or where a light fixture is in a room - those are your possible sources of light.

Use the light as a guide where to draw shading, so a circle can transform in a sphere. Amateur artists will just place shadows and highlights where they think it looks good, so then, the drawing will turn out looking wrong. It is not as simple as coloring in a drawing, especially when only working with grey pencils.

A drawing can also have multiple sources of light. The closer or stronger the light source is, the darker the shadows and the lighter the highlights will be. That is another reason why artists should start with drawing objects from the real world. Understanding how light affects how an object looks is important in accurately capturing it on paper. Always pay close attention to the object you are drawing, including the different factors that surround it.

17

Highlighting

Highlights are parts of an object where bright areas form as a light hits it. The part, which is most directly hit by the light source will then be the brightest, thus, you need to shade them with light values. This should be the portion closest to the light. An apple directly under a light bulb will have a highlight on its top portion that graduates as you move down to the bottom of the apple where you will find the shadow. As such, highlights accentuate the form of an object because it can depict where an object bulges or where parts of it protrude.

In portrait drawings, the highlights are often found on the tip of the nose, the apples of the cheeks, the forehead, the chin and the Cupid's bow. The texture of an object will also affect how highlights look on it. For instance, shiny surfaces like glass, water or a person's eyes will catch light better than coarser surfaces like sand, carpeting or wood. Also, the color of an object affects how well it can reflect light back to the viewer.

Light-colored or white-colored objects generally reflect light better while dark-colored objects absorb light, so light green leaves on a tree will have lighter highlights than the dark wood of its trunk. However, the contrast between the highlight and the rest of the object can also be more apparent in dark-colored objects. For instance, highlight on brunette hair is more obvious than on blond hair.

The value of a highlight also varies depending on the type of highlight that an object receives. A highlight formed from the direct light of a source should be bright. However, highlights can also form from indirect reflections or bouncing of light around the object. For example, the shiny surface of an apple can bounce a tiny bit of light on objects surrounding it. Their highlights will be faint, but these should still be depicted to create more realistic representations of the objects.

Casting Shadows

Shadows are found in the parts of a drawing that receive the least amount of light. It can also be found when parts of an object block the light such as in creases and dips. Things surrounding that object can also block light or cast a shadow depending on the angle that the light is coming from. These are then shaded with the darker values, so the top of an apple right under a bright light will still have dark shading where you can find the stem. In portrait drawings, shadows can be found on the parts of the face obscured by hair, the inside of the mouth, the cheekbones, under the eyebrows and eyes, and the creases in the ears, around the eyes and mouth.

Just like in highlighting, the natural color and texture of an object will also affect the shadows that form on it. For example, a long-haired fur coat on a dog will create a lot of small shadows where the tiny hairs are located. The shadow on a black t-shirt will also have to be much darker than when drawing shadows on a white t-shirt where it more easily shows up.

A shadow should also be graduated and should not simply appear as black shading. The portions of a shadow farther away from where an object obstruct light should be lighter, so the long shadow of a tree will be darkest near the roots and fade to a lighter value as it moves away from the roots. This also suggests the placement of objects in your drawing and creates the illusion of depth and perspective.

Shadows also suggest the parts of objects that are touching or are close to one another. Instead of drawing sharp edges, an object's edges can be more realistically depicted through the use of shadows.

Reflected light also affects how shadows look. The form of an object can be further enhanced by looking at where light is reflected from other objects. This goes in tandem with highlighting. Once you understand how highlighting and shadowing works, you can create three dimensional realities in your drawings.

Hatching

Hatching is a set of straight or curved lines drawn in a series beside each other to achieve a particular value. This is a common shading technique and is the easiest to master. That is because you are only working with one set of hatches. The density of the hatches will create the effect that you want, so hatching sets close to one another will look darker while hatching sets that are far apart will look lighter. Very close hatching lines will create the illusion of a solid value or color.

The hatches can also be short or long depending on the area that the artist wants to cover. For example, a shadow cast by a pine tree will form a triangular shape. So, the hatches can be a series of short and long lines that form the rough shape of a triangle. Hatching is also commonly used to draw straight hair or fur.

You can achieve graduation by changing the thickness of the lines and the distances between them. The principle is similar to some stroke techniques discussed in the previous chapter.

Crosshatching

Crosshatching is a type of hatching where the hatching sets are laid on top of one another as if creating crosses. When you overlap two or more hatching sets, you can create darker values. However, crosshatched sets with hatching sets that are far apart will show up as lighter values. The form of crosshatched sets usually follows the shape of an object to depict creases and textures. It is often used to show shadows on an object and does not have to rely on an outline. The spaces in between the hatches can be apparent or they can look like a solid shade depending on the effect that the artist wants to achieve.

Scribbling

Scribbling can also be a shading technique, especially when used in overlapping sets to create different values. It is a versatile technique that you can use to create shading on textures like curly hair, grassy fields or fuzzy cloth. The texture of scribbles can be adjusted to depict the smoothness or roughness of a surface. Scribbles and be a series of squiggles, entwined circles or irregular continuous lines. When used properly by more advanced artists, scribbling can still look quite polished rather than look like a random, unfinished doodle.

Dots

Dots are technically small lines or points. You can use them for shading through a variation of density and pressure. In essence, a densely grouped set of heavily drawn dots will look darker than a group of light dots drawn far apart. It does take a longer time to shade using dots than with other shading techniques, but the payoff can well be worth it. The illusion can be interesting for the viewer especially for larger art pieces. The nearer the viewer is, the more he or she will be able to appreciate the effort that went into the drawing.

A type of drawing that uses dots exclusively is called pointillism. Every dot is laid dot one by one to create lines, forms and shapes.

You can also cheat with this technique by holding several pencils together to draw multiple dots at the same time. It may be less precise, but it does cover more area in a shorter period of time. This technique is sometimes called stippling.

Chapter 6 - Easy Technique 3 - Proportion

Proportion is another important element of any good drawing. Many drawings with good lines and shading still look odd because they do not follow the right proportions. Think of a room filled with people. You may think that all the people in that room are the same size, so you will draw them that way. However, a room is not a flat like a piece of paper. People will stand in different places with some closer to the viewer than others, so those who are closest to you should look bigger than those standing in farther parts of the room.

Also, their sizes and shapes will depend on which direction of the room you are looking towards. If you are looking slightly upwards to the ceiling while sitting down on the floor, then the people's legs will look bigger than their heads, even though common sense dictates that legs should be smaller than heads. This distortion is due to different factors that affect proportion.

Depth of field

Any three dimensional drawing will have different depths of field. There should at least be a foreground, middle ground and background and objects should be found on these different levels. This tricks the viewer's eye into thinking that he or she is not looking at a flat piece of paper but rather, a 3-dimensional picture.

As such, the placement of objects on these different levels of depth of field will affect their size and shape. The objects closest to the viewer should appear biggest while the objects farthest from the viewer should appear smallest. Their sizes relative to one another in the drawing will also be affected by the distances between these levels and the actual sizes of the objects. For instance, a large mountain can still appear quite large even when it is in the background of a drawing, granted that the distance of the mountain is not that far from the viewer. A bird in the foreground will still look quite small compared to other objects in a landscape drawing because birds really are small in real life.

Foreshortening

Foreshortening refers to the shortening of an object as it moves towards the viewer. For instance, imagine a person with one arm by his side and another arm reaching out towards you. The arms on an average person should be the same length, but when drawing arms at different distances from the viewer, the arm closer to you should look shorter but bigger. This suggests that the arm is in the foreground while the other arm is located farther in the drawing.

The same principle applies when drawing any object that occupies different depths of field. For instance, you may be drawing a picture of a car from its front. The front of the car including its hood, front window and headlights should look big but short while its rear end should taper longer and look smaller.

By using foreshortening, you can also create the illusion of using different "lenses" in your drawing much like in photography. For example, a fish eye lens distorts an image in such a way that the center is larger and shorter than the rounded edges. You can use this when drawing reflections on concave surfaces like balls or windows or when depicting objects inside glasses like fishbowls and eyeglasses.

Similarly, wide-angle lenses also distort an image so that the central objects look large and shortened compared to the sides. You can use this technique when trying to depict objects that should look extremely close to the viewer like a very close-up shot of a person's face or a focal building surrounded by other minor buildings in an urban landscape.

Focal Point

The focal point is also important to consider when trying to get the perspective of a drawing correctly. This is the point where the viewer's eye is focused. Understand that your eyes can only point in one direction and on only one spot in a scene. That is why there are points in a scene that we call blind spots - spots that your eyes cannot see. To create realistic drawings, you can also mimic the illusion of peripheral vision.

To find the focal point of a drawing, just choose one spot to focus on in a scene. This can be found on any level of depth of field. However, beginner artists may want to start with a focal point somewhere in the middle ground or foreground and somewhere to one side of the scene. In a room, this can be the corner of one of the far walls. In a landscape, this can be the tip of a mountain. Also, take note that your focal point will be the focus of your drawing. It is one part where the eyes of the viewer will be drawn to, so choose a significant portion of the scene, usually one where the main subject is located.

Next, imagine lines radiating from that focal point. You can also draw these lines as your first layer of outlines as explained in Chapter 4. These lines will serve as guidelines for foreshortening your objects. Lines that radiate farther apart from one another should have shorter and bigger objects while lines that radiate closer to each other should contain longer and smaller objects.

Finding the focal point is much easier when drawing large scenes that contain different objects. It is a lot harder when drawing single subject accompanied by not a lot of objects. Sometimes, the focal point is already that one subject. This usually happens in portrait drawings, so just focus on one striking detail on the person's face like the lips or eyes then use shading and highlighting to emphasize that feature. It is always better to draw the viewer's gaze to one point in the drawing than to have a lot of things going on in a picture.

Grid Method

Drawing: 1-2-3 Easy Techniques to Mastering Drawing

For more accurate perspectives and scale, you can try the grid method when drawing. The grid method involves drawing as grid or a series of squares that will serve as guide when you are drawing a subject. These squares are of equal ratio and can be part of your first layer of outlines. They are usually erased before the drawing is finalized.

You can draw a rough grid on your paper by first finding the middle. Draw a vertical line and a horizontal line that meets in the middle of the paper, then divide the rest of the paper into equal parts. You can also use a ruler or straight edge to create a more precise guide. Some people may prefer to fold their paper in equal parts to create a sort of invisible grid without drawing any lines on the paper. However, you may find that the folds on the paper can still be distracting and may make it difficult to draw lines and shading more smoothly. This trick is best done on thin paper where folds can be smoothed out.

Then, imagine these lines over the subject you are drawing. They will allow you to find the correct placement of objects as well as their proper proportions relative to one another. It is best to start in the middle of the scene and work your way around the rest of the image. You are essentially filling out each box with a part of the image much like a jigsaw puzzle being put together. Be aware of the whole image that you are producing because if you focus on individual portions of the drawing without considering the bigger picture, the parts may end up looking disjointed.

This technique is especially useful in portrait drawings because the average human face has perfect proportions. The middle of the grid will be the nose and the eyes and mouth are located on equal distances from the nose.

Your grid does not necessarily have to be flat. It can also form the shape of a sphere as when drawing a round human head or a globe. Images that form cylinders or other curved objects will also benefit from a more spherical grid. The middle of spherical grids can be a straight line if the viewer is looking the image straight on or a curved line if the viewer is looking at an angle.

The grid technique is also used in image transfers. This is another exercise that beginner artists can try. You can do this by taking a printed photo and drawing a grid over the image, then try copying the image by drawing a similar grid on your paper and simply sketching the image as an exact replica of the photograph. This may not teach you how to draw realistically because you are drawing from another flat image, but it will teach you how to make use of the grid technique. It is also great when you want to simply copy other two-dimensional images like cartoons or letterings.

Over time and after a lot of practice, you can simply imagine the grid on your paper without having to draw it as an outline.

Conclusion

Thank you again for downloading this book!

I hope this book was able to help you to master basic techniques in drawing and help you on your way to becoming an advanced artist who experiments with different media and art genres.

The next step is to practice, practice and practice! That is the only way you can be a better artist. Try out every single tip you encountered in this book and draw wherever you can - at home, in a café, or out on the street. In no time, you will find that you rarely even think of these "rules" anymore and the lines, shading and proportion comes naturally to you as an artist.

Finally, if you enjoyed this book, please take the time to share your thoughts and post a review on Amazon. It'd be greatly appreciated!

Thank you and good luck!

Book 2
Pastel Drawing

By Scott Landowski

1-2-3 Easy Techniques to Mastering Pastel Drawing

Copyright 2017 by Scott Landowski - All rights reserved.

In no way is it legal to reproduce, duplicate, or transmit any part of this document in either electronic means or in printed format. Recording of this publication is strictly prohibited and any storage of this document is not allowed unless with written permission from the publisher. All rights reserved.

Table of Contents

Introduction

I want to thank you and congratulate you for downloading the book, "Pastel Drawing: 1-2-3 Easy Techniques to Mastering Pastel Drawing!"

This book contains proven steps and strategies on how to master the pastel medium to create stunning works of art. Art, in all its forms, plays an essential role in making our everyday lives more delightful, satisfactory and inspirational. It affects our mood in a positive way and brings a sense of tranquility that helps us get through some difficult and stressful times. Although art may not be a vital necessity, no one can deny the joy it brings.

Art is also a great way to express ourselves and to translate the beauty in nature that surrounds us. And one of the best forms we can translate it into is a beautiful piece of drawing or painting. Inspiration is everywhere, all that is left for artists to do is to grab a medium and start recording it. To achieve optimal results, what better medium can we use than pastels!

Pastels offer extremely vivid and intense colors that can make your drawings look realistic when done skillfully. The sense of fulfillment you will feel while viewing your finished artwork is undeniable. With the right amount of passion, patience and determination, anyone can master the art of pastel drawing and be an inspiration to others.

To help you achieve just that, this book will provide you with some easy tips, techniques and tutorials that you will surely find beneficial for your development. So, grab your pastels and paper and bring out your artistic side. Now is the best time to show off your pastel drawing skills!

Thanks again for downloading this book, I hope you enjoy it!

Chapter 1: What is a Pastel?

A pastel is an art medium made by mixing pure powdered pigment together with a binder to create a thick paste. The thick paste is then formed into sticks and allowed to dry. Because they are fashioned with almost pure and dry pigment, the color produced by pastels is richer and more intense than that of other art media.

Pastel is also the term used to describe an artwork—can be a drawing or a painting—created using pastel sticks. A "pastelist" is an artist who uses pastels as their medium in creating their artwork.

1.1. Types of Pastels

There are four general types of pastels: hard, soft, pencil, and oil. While they are all basically pigment in the form a stick, they differ in the way by which they are bound together. Hard pastels, soft pastels, and pastel pencils are held together with a water-based binder, usually a gum or resin. On the other hand, oil pastels are bound with an oil-based binder, usually oil or wax. This gives oil pastels a distinct texture comparable to oil paints.

Since hard, soft and pastel pencils are similarly bound, they are compatible with each other and can be worked on the same drawing or painting. Oil pastels, however, can only be worked with alone and cannot be combined with any other pastel types.

You can tell the distinction between these four pastel types by their look and texture.

Here are the main characteristics of each type:

Hard Pastels

Hard pastels contain less pigment and more binder than soft pastels. The more binder they have, the harder they become. This makes the color effect of hard pastels less intense. However, they do not crumble or crack as easily as soft pastels.

Hard pastels are usually cylindrical in shape and are hard and shiny. They can be sharpened using a knife to produce fine lines. Because they are firmer and more stable, hard pastels are particularly suitable for working on location and drawing techniques. Alternatively, the edges of hard pastel sticks can be used to apply extensive swathes of color.

Hard pastels are available in students' and artists' quality, and come in fewer colors than soft pastels. They can be used in blending, and are well-suited for working on small details, initial sketches and finishing touches.

Soft Pastels

Soft pastels, also called chalk pastels or "dry" pastels, are the most commonly used type of pastels. They have highly concentrated pigment that is bound together with the slightest amount of binder possible. The colors of soft pastels are delicately bright and intense. However, since they are dry and do not stick to the surface, they crumble easily and can be brushed off.

Soft pastels look and feel like typical blackboard chalk— soft and powdery with a cylindrical shape. This fragile consistency allows the artist to blend and layer various colors easily on the working surface. This also gives the artist prompt feedback on the colors as they apply them.

Soft pastels are best for beginners. If used with pastel pencils, soft pastels can help you create fine lines. As they are "chalky," you can make minor corrections or erasures which can be difficult to do with oil pastels.

With some manufacturers offering up to 500 colors, soft pastels have the widest selection of colors compared to other pastel types. They also come in a range of sizes: thick sticks, half sticks, and whole sticks.

Deciding between hard and soft pastels depends on the drawing techniques you'd like to make use of. If you're a beginner, you can begin mainly with soft pastels. Invest in a few individual hard pastels so you can try them out and use them for preliminary sketches and fine details.

Pastel Pencils

Pastel pencils are best if you want to create detailed and controlled artworks with pastels. They are versatile and can be used in combination with soft or hard pastels. You can use them wet or dry and they work well in blending technique. Pastel pencils can be sharpened to a point to draw precise and defined details. They are also recommended for basic sketching and drawing.

Pastel pencils look much like traditional pencils, but enclosed within the wood is a thin pastel stick with a consistency between soft and hard pastels. They are convenient to use as they are neat, unlike soft pastels. With pastel pencils, you can create quick sketches or drawings without much preparation or clean-up. This makes them suitable for working outdoors.

Oil Pastels

Oil pastels are like oil paints in terms of versatility and texture. But unlike oil paints, oil pastels don't have smelly chemicals and don't harden or dry out completely. As compared to soft pastels which produce more delicate and softer hue, oil pastels create brighter, more intense hue that makes them suitable for rough, bold and expressive work.

Oil pastels can also be worked, thinned, and diluted like oil paintings. They are round-shaped and have a wax-like, creamy consistency, making them easily distinguishable from soft pastels. They are also more stable and adhere to the working surface better than soft pastels.

Oil pastels do not require fixatives. They do not smudge, crumble, or release fine dust into the air which can result to respiratory irritation, whereas soft pastels often do. For this reason, and due to their non-toxic properties, oil pastels are the preferred type of pastel to be used in schools.

Oil pastels can also be great for beginners as it doesn't necessarily require setting up various solutions, brushes or other tools. All you need to get started are your oil pastel sticks and a sheet of paper to work on, and you're good to go.

Like other pastel types, oil pastels also come in either students' quality or artists' quality. Cheaper oil pastels have a look and feel like kids' crayons. They don't produce the same effect as artist quality pastels. This is frustrating to artists who are new to oil pastels and they often switch to other medium without discovering the real essence of oil pastels. So, if you're interested in trying out oil pastels, you need to be mindful of the difference between these two qualities. The difference alone could be the key factor in deciding whether you should continue using oil pastels.

1.2.   Drawing Materials

To get started with pastel drawing, all you basically need is a set of pastels and a pastel paper to work on. However, due to the wide selections of drawing materials available on the market, a beginner can get confused and overwhelmed. To help you out, here is a list of art materials you need and some buying tips:

A Set of Pastels

Although there are many different choices available, choosing a set of pastel is quite easy. When you use pastels in drawing, you don't really want to blend individual colors too much as they tend to lose their brilliance or vibrancy if you do. So, in choosing a set of pastels, you would want to get the largest set you can afford to buy, with the most number of colors. This is to reduce the frequency of blending you would have to do.

Another factor to consider is how the colors are grouped in the various sets. Choosing a set really depends on your subject taste. Some sets are grouped with colors that would be used for purposes such as for drawing landscapes, portraits, seascapes, and the like. Some sets consist of general colors.

Pastel Paper

The paper you need to use for pastel drawing needs to have the required roughness (called the paper's "tooth") on which the pastel will adhere. The surface of an ordinary writing paper is too smooth and it doesn't allow the pastel to grip onto it. So, in buying paper for pastel drawing, always choose paper that is manufactured specifically for pastel work.

Pastel papers are fashioned in various ways to give different levels of texture and tooth. You can experiment with several pastel papers with varying textures and tooth until you find the one that suits your taste best.

Other Drawing Materials

While pastel sticks and paper are the basic materials you need in drawing, there are also other art materials you can make use of to aid in achieving better results.

- Charcoal sticks for preliminary sketches and drawings

- A clean cloth or wet wipes for cleaning up

- Sand paper for layered/textured drawings

- Gloves for skin protection

- Brushes for special effects and blending

- Bread for erasures

- Pastel stick holder

- Cotton buds to blend small areas

- A blending stump or a tissue to blend tones and colors

- Craft knife to trim paper to desired size and for special effects

- For other special effects, you may use a soft eraser, a sponge and toilet paper

- A can of fixative spray to protect your artwork and prevent it from being ruined by careless smudging (a hair spray can also be used as an alternative)

1.3.   Pastel Quality

Pastels, like other art media, come in different levels of quality. Generally, there are two main pastel grades: students' quality and artists' quality. Students' quality pastels are less expensive and usually have low quality pigments. They are also made with more binder and filler which make the colors less intense and vibrant. However, they do not easily crumble like artist grade pastels. Artists' quality pastels, on the other hand, contain stronger and more tightly-bound pigments. The pigment and binder are more proportional which makes the color bolder and more intense. Artists' quality pastels also have a wider selection of colors and are more fade-resistant than student grade pastels.

Beginners and intermediate artists who are not yet willing to invest in more expensive quality pastels can begin with the students' set. But if you are serious about pastel drawing, buy the artists' quality pastels and you will see a great difference with the results.

1.4.   Pastel Colors

You can blend pastel colors but you cannot mix them as well as you can with paint. To make up for this, a wide range of colors is made available on the market. You can purchase pastels individually or in sets. If you're a beginner and unsure as to which pastel type you want to invest in, you can begin by getting yourself individual pastels which will also keep your expenses low. Once you have figured which type you really want to buy, you can get a set of pastels that contains a good range of colors. You can also choose and customize your own set of colors.

Some artist grade pastels contain rare pigments which make them costlier than others. Alternatively, some student grade pastels contain artificial pigments which imitate the color of the more expensive natural pigments. If you see the word "hue" after the pigment name, it means that the pigment of the pastel is made using a cheaper substitute.

1.5.   Health and Safety

Pastels, especially soft pastels, are a dry medium and often deposit airborne dust which you can inhale as you work. This dust can cause respiratory discomfort and can be quite dangerous. To avoid inhaling pastel dust, work in a well-ventilated room. You can also wear face masks or get an air purifier to make you less exposed to dust.

Some pastels also contain toxic pigments like cadmium. Exposure to cadmium can lead to cadmium poisoning. To avoid this, buy only non-toxic pastels which are available at any local art supply store.

Chapter 2: Techniques for Pastel Drawing

The techniques for pastel drawing can be quite difficult to master especially for beginners. Unlike in painting, you cannot test the colors on a palette first before applying them to the surface, but rather you mix and blend the medium directly on the drawing surface. Also, en error in pastel drawing cannot be concealed the way an error in painting can be painted out.

Anyhow, there are various ways by which you can apply pastels to a surface. Some of these techniques can help you get away with errors. There is no right or wrong way in carrying out these techniques. You should simply select the technique that is most appropriate for your desired effect. For most pastel drawings, you can use these techniques in combination with each other.

2.1.   Blending

Blending is probably the most common and basic technique for pastel drawing. Blending happens when different pastel colors are applied in layers on the same area. You can smooth the transition between tones and colors by rubbing or smearing the pastel into the drawing surface. You can accomplish this using your finger, a tissue, blending stump, soft brush or cotton swab. You can use your finger for blending on large areas. But for smaller areas, use a blending stump or ear buds instead.

When you blend, and rub over the colors, you will notice that their vibrancy tends to diminish. Here is a way to overcome this: once you have blended the colors with your finger or a stump, gently rub the original colors on top of them to create a thin vibrant layer. This will help maintain the vibrancy of the pastel and achieve better results.

2.2.   Scumbling

Scumbling is a pastel technique in which thin but opaque layers of pastel are applied over the top of previously worked areas. This creates a partial covering and allows bits of the pastel underneath the new color to shine through. This technique produces visually stimulating results and is often used when working with landscapes and other natural scenes and objects.

When scumbling is done, the overlapping colors visually "mix" and cause the viewer to perceive a new color. This is often referred to as *optical color mixing*. For instance, if blue streaks are applied next to, or over yellow streaks, it creates a perception of green.

As you have imagined, the tooth or texture of the paper is one of the factors that affect the process of scumbling. So, to achieve the desired effect of scumbling, consider the tooth or texture of the paper that you will use.

2.3. Stippling

Stippling is a common drawing technique used to create areas of light and shade by dotting the medium down onto the working surface. This process is repeated until the desired effect is created. The more compressed the dots are, the darker the area will be. This technique works well in painting as well as in pastel drawing. It can also be done with other drawing media such as charcoal, crayons, and conte crayons.

Stippling can create an optical illusion when done by a skilled artist. From a distant view, the areas in which the shading was created will look like a smooth application of pastels. The dots will only be apparent when surveyed very closely.

2.4. Hatching

Hatching has 6 basic forms: *parallel hatching, contour hatching, cross hatching, fine cross hatching, tick hatching,* and *woven hatching*. Hatching techniques are used to create value, texture and the optical illusion of light and form by drawing lines close together in similar or various directions. Aside from pastels, these linear techniques also work well with many other drawing media such as colored pencils, graphite, and pen and ink. Hatching can also be observed in traditional techniques for printmaking such as engraving and etching.

Parallel Hatching

Parallel hatching is a basic form of hatching that uses non-crossing lines to demonstrate the value (light and shadow) on or round an object in a drawing. Hatching consists of sets of parallel lines positioned closely together. The areas where you place hatching will appear shaded and darker, and the areas where you don't will give the impression of a featured highlight.

Contour Hatching

Instead of using simple parallel lines, it is sometimes necessary to curve the lines and adhere to the contours of an object. This is referred to as *contour hatching*. In addition to creating value, contour hatching technique also enhances the volume and dimensionality of the object you are drawing.

Cross Hatching

After drawing one set of lines, you may add another set of lines on top to add more value to your hatching. The second set of lines can be drawn diagonally or perpendicularly to the first set, and can be another set of parallel lines of curved lines to adhere to the contours of the object. This cross-hatching technique is an effective way to create density variations and to deepen the values in your drawing.

Fine Cross Hatching

Fine cross hatching is the richest and most delicate hatching technique. It is done using the same method as above, consisting of various layers of cross hatching instead of only two, to create more gradations in value and tone. In fine cross hatching, a fine-line pencil or the edge of a hard-pastel stick is best used to draw more detailed and precise lines that will seem to blend together when viewed from far away.

Tick Hatching

Tick hatching is composed of short parallel marks or "ticks" that are piled over one another to produce variations in density. This technique works best with a broader pen or pastel to enhance the graphic quality of your drawing.

Woven Hatching

Woven hatching is also referred to as *basket hatching*. This technique provides very striking effects and enhances the graphic quality of your work when done correctly. To do this technique, draw a short set of parallel lines in the same direction, then another set of parallel lines in an almost-perpendicular or diagonal direction. The effect of this technique will look woven (thus the name) when used correctly. The marks can also be cross-hatched to create more density and achieve your desired effect.

2.5. Scratching

The technique of scratching gives your drawings added details that are simple but unique. To do this, lay down two or more contrasting colors before doing the main drawing. The greater the number of colors you lay, the greater the range of colors that will be revealed upon scratching. The result is more effective if the color of the final layer on top is dark. To do the scratching part, you need to make use of a scratching tool. It can be a needle, a painting knife, or a comb. If you don't have any of these tools, you can also sharpen your pastel stick to a point and use it to scratch out the image.

2.6. Feathering

Feathering is a drawing technique that usually uses layers of short strokes that may overlap or cross on top of each other. The lines that are drawn may also curve to adhere to the contours of an object in your drawing, and this adds to the illusion of light and form. Like scumbling, feathering can also provide vibrancy to your work, and result to optical color mixing in which the colors are visually mixed instead of being physically blended on the drawing surface.

This technique is particularly good for providing the glistening appearance of feathers, scales, and fabric, or for creating effects that are distinctive with light.

2.7. Other Tips and Techniques

There are three ways to use a pastel: by drawing with the end, the edge, or the side. Hold the pastel stick as you would hold a pen or pencil and it will create a great expression that suggests a sense of the gesticulation you made. You can vary the breadth of the line by applying alternate pressure to the pastel. The more pressure you apply, the more pastel you will be laying down on the surface. To create thinner lines, apply the pastel more lightly on the paper or you can also use the edge of the stick.

For detail work, you can create finer lines using the sharp edge of a new pastel stick. When it becomes blunt through use, you can re-sharpen it with a cutter or knife. You can also reshape the pastel stick by scraping it against a rough surface such as sandpaper. While most artists use pastel pencils to create more precise lines, learning this technique helps especially when you don't have a pencil available and need to draw finer marks.

If you want to create broad streaks of color quickly, you can draw with the side of the stick. For better results, split the stick in two and use one half of it. Alter the pressure to produce varying gradations of texture on the paper. When the side of the stick has eroded due to constant use, it will leave two sharp edges which you can then use to draw finer lines.

As previously mentioned, you can use a combination of any of these techniques in the same drawing. It is necessary to incorporate various strokes and marks in any image. Regardless of which technique/s you use, the goal is to always create established layers of various colors on the pastel paper. This provides depth in your work and enhances the illusion of light and form. Practice these easy techniques to further develop your artistic skills and to create successful pieces of pastel artwork.

Chapter 3: Basic Tips and Tutorials

Pastels can be a challenging medium to master. Their loose characteristic makes it difficult to control on the drawing surface. For this reason, beginners are often discouraged that they tend to dismiss this medium after only a few tries and move on to something else. This is unfortunate as many new artists miss out on the opportunity of discovering how great pastels can be. They shun the medium that might have been perfect for them if only they worked with it a little longer.

So, if you're new to pastels, keep working and don't limit yourself. Pastel drawing can be fulfilling. You can even discover new techniques of your own as you move along. Having said that, here are some basic tutorials, as well as some tips, to get you started with the amazing world of pastel drawing.

3.1.   Landscapes

One of the most common subjects of artists for their drawings are landscapes, and it is no wonder. As artists, we are moved by the natural beauty that surrounds us and interpreting them into beautiful works of art is the least we can do. Landscapes are overflowing with interesting shapes, lines, and varied colors. These elements often arrange themselves into visually appealing compositions and the artist will simply need to record them in the form of a drawing or a painting.

Pastels are inherently loose which makes them the perfect medium for interpreting natural sceneries such as landscapes. In this tutorial, we will record a typical, natural landscape with the use of soft pastels. Work on an orange pastel paper that has a rough texture (tooth) as this tutorial calls for heavy layering. The heavy tooth of the surface allows you to apply multiple layers of color without upsetting the tooth. This is essential for the coherent reception of the material.

Moving on, here are the steps in creating a beautiful landscape artwork:

- To begin, work a layer of darker blue over a layer of lighter blue pastels. This will form the background of the landscape. The light blue pastel creates the outlines for the clouds and develops the transition from light to dark. Use your finger to gently blend the colors of the clouds.

- Create a line for the distant row of trees. This should overlap the background. Apply a dark yellow-green pastel to begin. Then apply burnt umber followed by a light mark of black. Blend the colors gently with your finger and leave a hard edge on top of the row of trees.

- Next, to form the distant ground, use a variety of yellow-greens, followed by yellow-ochre, light cream, and a few bands of Burnt Sienna. This creates shapes of color that are aligned horizontally.

- Add several distant trees. Do not worry about the details. Instead, focus on the values, shapes and colors that are created.

- Apply a fair amount of light cream into the middle ground and allow tiny portions of the orange pastel paper to show through. Apply a few bands of burnt sienna for added color.

- Still working on the middle ground, apply patches of red over layers of purple, then darken it with burnt umber. This will form the grasses for the landscape. Use dark yellow-green pastel to draw smaller grasses and highlight it with a lighter yellow-green.

- Continue adding some more details to the image such as formations of rocks with small trees and bits of grass behind them. As you reach the closer ground or the foreground, make the lines for the grass longer and more precise. Use different colors and create variations in value to make your drawing appear more animated.

- Draw additional strokes with light cream pastel to imply the field of grass. Leave some recesses to reveal portions of the darker layers' underneath. You can also use a lighter cream pastel to highlight the tips of the taller grass blades.

- Going back to the background, grab a white pastel to intensify the colors of the clouds. Gently blend the new colors with the previously applied colors using your finger.

Your landscape drawing is now complete! You can finish off your work by spraying fixative all over it. You can also use a hairspray as an alternative. Fixative spray protects your work and prevents it from smudging.

3.2. Seascapes

Your repertoire as an artist will not be complete if you are not able to draw seascapes. This subject matter can be tricky as oceans are continually moving and your drawing needs to capture that illusion for it to be successful. Additionally, it can be quite difficult to draw if your target is always moving.

If you're a beginner, you can start with an image reference as an alternative. Learn and understand the basics of creating the illusion of waves and you can draw them easily. For seascapes, the same with landscapes, it is recommended to use a surface that has a heavy tooth as this subject often requires substantial applications of layering. You can use soft, hard or oil pastels, depending on your preference. As you move along, apply these tips to achieve appealing and desirable results:

- Scrutinize the subject very closely and you will be able to identify the directional lines, as well as the colors, values and tones being used. These elements are all essential to create the effect you are after. Place colors and values in the right locations within your drawing to give the viewer the illusion that they are seeing actual waves.

- Consider the sequence in which you are to draw the subject. Typically, pastelist commence the drawing by working on the background. Then develop the middle ground and foreground over the accomplished background. In this manner, you will be able to layer the colors in a more effective way.

- Create a great extent of value (the lightness and shadiness of a color) within your drawing. Value plays a vital role in the way we perceive things. Use different tones and shades from the same color group and it will help you achieve the illusion you're trying to make. For instance: although the ocean is generally blue, use other tones such as blue-green, green, dark blue, light blue and so on. Layer these colors and their values and it will aid in creating the illusion of moving water.

- Another important factor to consider is the directional lines. Since we are working with waves, observe the contrast between horizontal and diagonal lines. These are examples of contour lines for which you can use the layering techniques you have learned so far.

- Apply your medium in a manner that it adheres to the curves and contours which characterize the subject. Work with the contours of the waves to effectively bring about the effect you're after.

Due to its simplicity and seemingly unvarying color, the ocean might look like a simple thing to draw. But the challenge is to capture the illusion of movement and gleam of the waves within your drawing, and drive the viewer into believing that the waves are moving. With a little practice and enhancement of skills, you will eventually be able to pull it off quite easily.

3.3. Clouds

Another basic subject that a pastelist should master is the clouds. Landscapes and other scenes often require the presence of the sky. While a cloudless and still sky is easier to accomplish, —only some basic blending and layering of the medium will be enough—a scene that calls for clouds can become more complicated. Here are few useful tips to help you create more realistic-looking clouds.

- When you are drawing clouds, the first thing you should remember is that clouds are three-dimensional objects. Consequently, they will often have a shaded part and a highlighted part. It is essential to create the illusion of shadows and highlights to produce more natural and realistic clouds.

- Clouds take on various forms and shapes. This gives you the freedom to be loose and diverse when you're making the outlines of the marks. Exercise this freedom as this will promote the illusion and effect of organic shapes.

- As with most subject matters, it is important to observe value. Endeavor to incorporate a greater extent of value in any of your drawings. As clouds are often blue and white, you can use other tones such as gray, dark blue, light blue and the like, to create the illusion of three-dimensionality and dynamism.

These tips are important to remember not only for clouds, but for all types of subject matters. Apply these tips and in no time, you will master the creation of realistic-looking clouds.

Landscapes, seascapes and clouds may seem basic, but pulling them off convincingly requires skills and thorough understanding of the art. Exercise your creativity and adroitness in every artwork you are working on. With a good selection of medium and application of techniques, you can turn from a novice pastelist to a competent and skillful artist.

Chapter 4: Portrait Drawing with Pastels

Portrait drawing is a traditional art form. After all, what better subject can an artist have but themselves and the people around them? Whether you're drawing a self-portrait, a portrait of a loved one, or a stranger's perhaps, there are two main factors you should be mindful about: the proportions of the human face and the accuracy of your drawing to those proportions. In this chapter, we will study the basic rules of symmetry for the human face, which all pastelist, painters and artists alike must learn and understand. The other sections will provide you with simple approaches to drawing realistic eyes, nose, lips and ears.

4.1. Understanding Facial Proportions

Drawing a portrait is rather like drawing any other types of subject matter. You must scrutinize the subject so that you can draw the features accurately. The goal is to always make the closest resemblance possible between the portrait and the subject. To do this, it is important to understand facial proportions first.

Proportion is the relation of one part to another or to the whole with respect to placement and size. Generally, human faces follow the same rules of symmetry but many people still make mistakes when drawing the human face due to their lack of understanding of the facial symmetry. When drawing a face, follow these basic rules to get the job done correctly:

- First thing to keep in mind is that the eyes are always found in the middle of the face. People tend to make mistakes on this and incorrectly position the eyes way up the forehead. You can draw a horizontal line halfway in the middle of the face to serve as the "eye line" and position the eyes there.

- Typically, the width of a human face is five times the width of a single eye. Of course, you need to draw only two eyes. The concept of "five eyes" should serve as a guide to help you determine the correct width of the face.

- When drawing a line for the nose, it should run from the center of the eye line down to the bottom of the face. When drawing the actual nose, it should be thinnest between the eyes and growing a bit wider down the nostrils. There are exceptions to this, of course. Obviously, everyone has a unique nose. Some noses are longer, some are wider, some are thinner, and so on. So, you really need to pay attention to the details of your subject's nose to capture it more accurately.

- Each inside corner of the eyes typically aligns with either edge of the nose, while each pupil of the eyes typically aligns with either corner of the mouth.

- The line for the mouth runs from the center of the nose line down the bottom of the face. This line indicates the location where the top and bottom lip meet.

- Typical ears are positioned between the nose line and the eye line.

Keep these simple basics in mind and use them as a guide to help you draw a properly proportioned face. Most importantly, study the face of your subject carefully to get more precise results. These are only standard rules that may be applicable to most people, but not to everyone.

4.2. Drawing the Eye

As the saying goes, eyes are the windows to the soul. Amongst all facial features, the eyes are the most expressive. When you're drawing the subject's eyes, it will be more convincing if you can resemble not only the physical characteristics of the eyes but also the emotions that may hide behind them. To draw an eye that looks realistic, here is a step-by-step approach:

- To begin, sketch the outlines of the shape of the eye using a skin-tone color first, then a dark brown.

- Layer the colors in the iris of the eye. Apply green, blue, and a bit of yellow then blend the colors with your finger.

- Next, layer the darker values and tones of the iris over the initial colors. You can use blue and dark brown for this. Layering is always essential in any drawing. It creates depth and makes the colors look more convincing and realistic.

- Apply additional colors directly upon the darker layer, but this time, less mixing and smudging is needed. You can use light blue and yellow-green for this.

- Highlight some of the areas in the iris part of the eye with a light cream. You can also use this color in the white areas of the eyes.

- Apply some marks with red, cream, and red-orange. This is to indicate the edges of the eye.

- Layer white on top of the slightly darker values of the white areas of the eye. This creates a highlight and makes the eye look moist. You can also use white on top of the iris to make it look "sparkly."

- Apply skin-tone colors round the eye. Work the colors into the surface as you apply them.

- Continue to add and blend the skin-tone colors into the working surface.

- Finally, add the eyelashes with a black pencil. A nicely sharpened pastel pencil will create more precise-looking eyelashes.

Your realistic eye drawing is now complete! As always, a careful study of your subject's facial features should be done to make the finished work more accurate.

4.3. Drawing the Nose

Drawing noses is easier than you may think. Many people seem to struggle with this part but it's rather simple. Here are the basics:

- To begin, draw four curved lines: two lines for the nostrils, two lines for the edges of the nose.

- Apply darker values on the shaded areas of the nose. Begin with the darkest areas then to the midtones. You can do this with a pencil first.

- Continue to add shading on the right locations of the nose to make the illusion that there is a source of light. Do not add more marks or lines. Focus on shading the dark areas while leaving some of the areas slightly untouched.

- Adding more value will make your nose look more realistic. Light areas of the nose will appear protruded, while the dark areas will look like they're way at the back.

- Look for the light and dark areas on your subject's nose and draw them as you see them. By doing this, your nose will appear lifelike.

Isn't that easy? All you need to draw are four simple lines and the rest is shading and adding value. As for the shape, size and length of the nose, it really depends on your subject. There is no specific formula when it comes to drawing noses, you should observe your subject closely and draw the specifications that you will see.

4.4. Drawing the Lips

Some people seem to have problems when it comes to drawing the lips or mouth. This is mainly because everyone has a unique set of lips. So, there is no definite method for drawing the lips but there are some things you can consider that may make the task easier.

- Observation is the key. Every set of lips is different. Whether your subject is a live person or from a photo reference, it is always important to scrutinize each feature to get the exact size, shape, color and curves of the lips.

- Use contour lines to aid in outlining the shape of the lips. Also, apply the layering techniques you have learned from the previous chapters to make the lips look believable. Apply the pastels onto the working area using contour lines, as well.

- At the beginning, it is okay to be loose with your drawing. Forming the shape of the lips might call for some mistakes and that is fine, so long as you get the correct form. Especially when you're using soft pastels, you can remedy the mistakes later. Keep your working area clean but do not worry too much about stray lines and marks.

- Pastel drawing requires several layering, particularly with soft pastels. You may need to do more layering to get the result that you want so don't get frustrated if your work doesn't look developed enough after only a few layers. Establish the colors and always keep your cool.

4.5. Drawing the Ears

As with all facial features, ears vary in sizes and shapes. Pay close attention to the shapes and lines of your subject's ears and draw them exactly as you see them. Drawing realistic ears is simple. You only need to draw the outlines or contours of your subject's ears and the rest is shading and adding value (same as with drawing noses). As there is no definite formula regarding drawing ears, remember these basic tips instead to accomplish the job more effectively:

- Be familiar with the proper location of the ears. As discussed earlier, ears are typically positioned between the nose line and the eye line. Be careful not to place them way below the nose or way above the eyes as they will not look properly proportioned if you do.

- Keep in mind that every set of ears is unique, as all facial features are. Learn to analyze and examine even the subtlest details that are present on every subject and from every angle. Little details can make a difference with the outcome.

- Remember that ears are complementary features of the portrait—they are not the main subject. Sometimes, the ears are completely or partially covered either by the subject's hair or any other accessory the subject may be wearing. Do not become too preoccupied with working with the ears that you overlook the whole picture.

Drawing the facial features often follow the same basic rules. And in all your drawings, never miss to observe each feature of your subject's face to capture its unique specifics.

Hopefully by now you have already drawn a realistic portrait with all the facial features properly positioned. As you will notice, one great thing about the pastel medium is that it gives the artists the best of both worlds. Although we generally call it "drawing," the results often look like they are "painted" instead of drawn. This is due to the vivid and vibrant colors that pastels often contain. In fact, pastel-drawn artworks are usually called "painting."

Now that you have learned the basics of portrait drawing with pastels, why don't you invite a friend or a loved one to become the subject for your drawings? A truly skillful artist can not only draw a good portrait that resembles the subject, but can also capture the character and personality of the subject in their drawings. Now this may sound too demanding but with a creative mind and passionate will, the possibilities are limitless!

Chapter 5: An Overview of Still Life Drawing

Although it may not always be the most interesting subject, drawing still life can be quite exciting. It is good practice for developing and enhancing observational skills, as well as interpretative skills of an artist. With still life, you can learn how to perceive objects like an artist—with a mindful awareness of their shape, tone, texture, color, form, outline, proportions and composition.

5.1. What is Still Life?

But what really is still life? To say simply, still life is an arrangement or a scene of inanimate objects that are either painted or drawn from observation. Still life arrangement can be composed of related or unrelated objects. The goal is to create an artwork that is skillfully constructed, thought provoking and aesthetically pleasing.

Contrary to landscape painting or drawing, still life subjects give artists more freedom to create the picture and decide on its compositions before painting or drawing anything. Traditionally, objects that comprise still life arrangements include foods, flowers, glasses, bottles and vases. Some modern artists, however, have averted from tradition and they are more liberated in choosing their subjects.

5.2. The Rule of Odds

The Rule of Odds applies to all forms of visual arts—photography, sculpture, graphic design and painting. This rule states that objects grouped together will look more interesting and appealing if they have an odd number. Viewers, for some reason, would rather look at a composition of "3" objects instead of "2," or "5" rather than "4."

The human eye has the tendency to wander to the middle of the group. If it sees an even number of objects, it will end up looking at the blank center and this inhibits eye movement.

When composing a still life arrangement, strive to apply the Rule of Odds to achieve a more aesthetically pleasing composition. If you have one main object, complement it with two or four supporting objects so one of them will be the center.

Still life has given artists a platform to explore their association with the objects that exist in their world. Practice drawing with still life objects to improve your techniques and further develop your skills as an artist.

Conclusion

Thank you again for downloading this book!

I hope this book could unleash the artist in you and inspire you to become a better, more competent pastel list.

The possibilities with respect to creating art are seemingly endless! In our world filled with beauty and wonder, you will never run out of inspiration. The marvelous scenes of nature, the picturesque views of our surroundings, and the smiles of our loved ones are all too inciting not to draw and capture every moment of.

But art isn't only about interpreting the world in which we live in. It is also a great way to express our inner thoughts and feelings about life. Our dreams, memories, longings, fears and joy can also be translated into wondrous artworks. Art is a means of self-expression that lets the audience peek into the world within us. What a nice feeling it is when you can just let everything out!

Everywhere we go, art is evident, inspiring us in many ways, influencing us to become a better person. It is amazing to know that with only a piece of paper in hand and a simple medium such as a pastel, we can pay tribute to all the beautiful things that life has given us, in a creative and passionate way.

Now, the next step is to keep moving forward. Practice your pastel drawing skills and never be afraid to take it to the next level. If at first you don't achieve the result that you want, do not dwell on the frustration and do better next time. A pastel drawing master was once a beginner who failed but didn't give up. Keep pushing yourself to the limit. Do not hold back. Be bolder. Let your creativity overflow. Who knows, you might just one day be lined up with all the world's greatest pastel artists!

Finally, if you enjoyed this book, please take the time to share your thoughts and post a review on Amazon. It'd be greatly appreciated!

Thank you and good luck!

www.ingramcontent.com/pod-product-compliance
Lightning Source LLC
Chambersburg PA
CBHW071827170526
45167CB00003B/1453

* 9 7 8 1 5 4 2 7 8 2 7 4 6 *